WORCESTER
PAST & PRESENT

RAY JONES

SUTTON PUBLISHING

Sutton Publishing Limited
Phoenix Mill · Thrupp · Stroud
Gloucestershire · GL5 2BU

First published 2001

British Library Cataloguing in Publication Data
A catalogue record for this book is available from the
British Library.

ISBN 0-7509-2771-2

Typeset in 10.5/13.5 Photina.
Typesetting and origination by
Sutton Publishing Limited.
Printed and bound in England by
J.H. Haynes & Co. Ltd, Sparkford.

Worcester bridge in flood, as seen from the Cathedral tower
(4 November 2000).

CONTENTS

INTRODUCTION

Like many towns and cities in Britain Worcester is undergoing constant change. Endless debate takes place on whether or not such change is always desirable or necessary, but, despite never-ending public enquiries and planning hurdles to be jumped, the townscape of our city seems to be changing beyond recognition.

The population of Worcester continues to grow – from a city of 11,001 inhabitants in 1779, to 33,226 in 1871, to 46,624 in 1901, and now to over 90,000; the rate of expansion has increased greatly. In years gone by the principal causes of changing a townscape were natural and largely unmonitored population growth, and the relative prosperity and success of the city defining size and structure. However, in more recent years, as a direct result of planning policies, the population has been artificially increased by the provision of brand-new housing and industrial estates. I feel that it should concern us all that government can now dictate the future growth of our towns and cities; there is surely an optimum size for many of the historic population centres in this country and we should all be able to influence our local environment.

The city has not only changed internally – it has grown considerably in size from a mere 293 acres in 1779, taking in established settlements at Barbourne and St John's and stretching out beyond these areas. More recently it has sprawled relentlessly out towards the M5 motorway to engulf the historic hamlet of Trotshill, while recent attempts to build an identifiable ring road have also brought the inevitable infill. Covering ancient fertile farmlands with concrete may also have unexpected side-effects. It has been suggested that the devastating floods of late 2000 were worse because of the lack of meadows to absorb the heavy rainfall. Obviously, much of Worcester's urban growth has been desirable in order to drive the city forward, but many changes have been poorly thought out, and were often unnecessary. As a result of this, the historic townscape has been considerably diminished. Most people will remember the awful mistakes of the 1960s when large parts of Worcester's historical heart were demolished in order to make way for bland concrete abominations, of which Lychgate was perhaps the worst. Lack of concern for conservation, however, was not a new concept. The Guesten Hall was, perhaps, the Lychgate of the nineteenth century. It was part of a number of monastic buildings to the south of the Cathedral and dated back to 1320; but, for the sake of around £1,000-worth of repairs, it was destroyed in 1860 amid a sea of apathy. The Guildhall, too, could well have met a similar fate in the 1870s when debate raged over replacement or repair. Thankfully, common sense eventually secured the future of one of the finest pieces of architecture in the city, but it was a close-run thing.

Now we have a situation where planners and councillors think they fully understand the importance of heritage, but, nevertheless, many old buildings disappear from the Worcester landscape every year. One area for optimism is that new buildings do seem to blend in with their surroundings in a much more pleasing fashion. The Countess of Huntingdon's Chapel, for example, seems perfectly at home with its modern Crowngate neighbours.

The shaping of our city still relies on inadequate local financial resources, the ownership of land, and, often crucially, the financial clout and influence of big business. Transportation policy remains unimaginative and unconcerned of its effect on local business. Costly and largely empty bus lanes threaten the viability of small shops and guest houses that line their route because of the unnecessary removal of parking spaces. Thoughts of using our local railway network do not seem to gather support because of the envisaged cost. Why are vast new estates to the east of our city totally reliant on the car when the priority is seemingly to reduce road traffic? No thought was given to the necessity of providing quick and easy access to the city centre from these new clusters of growth. To plan a city in tune with the requirements of the new century, while retaining its identity and attraction as a tourist centre, requires vision and money. It can still be done; let us hope for greater imagination from the people fortunate to be able to decide the future for us.

This book will examine some of the features of the townscape and its hinterland, and how they have changed, or not changed, during the twentieth century. Having chosen a number of relatively rare postcards and photographs from my archive I was faced with the considerable task of photographing these locations as they are now. This was not as easy as I had thought as I had not considered the influence of an unknown enemy – the tree. Many interesting or even beautiful vistas of bygone years are now obscured by a mass of green for large parts of the year. The centre of our city seems very pleasant during summer months as we walk along traffic-free roadways planted with trees and shrubs, but when you look upwards to enjoy the Georgian and Victorian façades that still can be discerned in many streets you find that they are hidden. I have no objection to a greener inner city environment, but it needs closer monitoring and cropping than currently exercised. I was relieved to note that I was not alone in my thinking when a letter entitled 'Visibility of Cathedral is important' appeared in our local paper recently: this commented on the poor visibility of the Cathedral from the High Street when the leaves of the trees are fully out both in the Cathedral grounds and the High Street. The writer surmised that the main reason for building the High Street at right angles to the Cathedral was for the view of the Cathedral thus obtained.

Trees also bring birds and their associated problems (pigeons are a particular health hazard). Is the predominant sound of an inland city on quiet Sunday mornings really the squawk of the seagull? Mind you, the clattering sound of approaching skateboards must come a close second!

Some of the views in this book may well be familiar, but they have been included in order to make comparisons. Nevertheless, I am pleased to include many photographs that have not been seen before in print. In general the modern photographs have been fairly closely matched to historic predecessors, but I have not been too pedantic in this approach as interesting aspects of change would then have been omitted. Unfortunately, those dreaded trees obscured direct comparisons in some cases, while modern traffic made some camera positions positively precarious.

All of the photographs in this book are from my own collection. Background information has been gathered from a wide variety of sources, including:

Bridges, T., and Mundy, C., *Worcester – A Pictorial History* (1996)
Gwilliam B., *Old Worcester: People and Places* (1993)
Morris, R.K., and Hoverd, K., *The Buildings of Worcester* (1994)
Various trade directories and Michael Grundy's 'Memory Lane' features.

Further information about the photographs in this book, including references to similar photographs in previous publications and details of the Parkbarn archive, may be found in the local history section of my website at: **http://www.surfworcester.co.uk**

Since the publication of my last book two of my greatest friends in the world of photography and postcards have sadly passed away. Michael Dowty, a prominent and perceptive photographer who was a great inspiration to me, died in 1999. John Brettell died later the same year, a very kind man whom I had the pleasure of knowing since the late 1970s when we had first met in the pet food trade. We shared a common interest in old postcards and local history. John and Michael are a great loss to the world of nostalgia.

Worcester before the flood as seen from the Cathedral tower. (September 2000)

1

The City Centre

The centre of Worcester is still, broadly speaking, the area of the city as it would have been at the turn of the nineteenth century (there was some linear growth along the Tything while St John's was virtually a separate village). Consequently, if you can ignore the more modern buildings and façades, there is still a sense of a city composed largely of eighteenth- and nineteenth-century brick buildings. Worcester's associations with the Elizabethan and Civil War periods are not so easily recalled visually, apart from the Friar Street and New Street areas. Old historic buildings, such as the Commandery and the Queen Elizabeth's House, are largely isolated within a newer streetscape.

The above photograph of St Andrew's gardens in September 2000 looks to the new millennium. However, the swansong of St Andrew's as a church was back in 1950 when demolition of most of the church took place. This was not that surprising as St Andrew's, once the most densely populated area in Worcester, had seen most of its houses bulldozed away in previous years. (September 2000)

The Cathedral on an early Edwardian postcard published by W.W. Harris. The architecture and majesty of this edifice could be fully appreciated from the High Street at this time. The surrounding railings were suitably impressive.

This view of the Cathedral gives the impression that the authorities wish the building to remain hidden by a magnificent array of mature trees. War memorials vie with the trees for attention. (September 2000)

The South African War Memorial on a postcard
published by W.W. Harris. It was unveiled on
3 September 1908, some six years after the end of
the second Boer War.

The South African War Memorial now dominates the
view as large trees obscure the Cathedral. I presume
that the ornate railings bordering the Cathedral green
were torn down in about 1940 in order to help the war
effort. The post box has changed shape and location.
(September 2000)

An Edwardian postcard by the Rotary Postcard Company of Edward Elgar (1857–1934). Although the very nature of Elgar's profession sentenced him to much time spent indoors, he was essentially an outdoors person as suggested by this study. Elgar took up cycling in 1900 and it rapidly became one of his favourite activities. This is probably my favourite photograph of one of our most famous citizens.

Elgar's 'Saturday Night and Sunday Morning'. Unfortunately not everyone regards Sir Edward with due reverence. Saturday night revellers had placed a traffic cone on the head of Worcester's greatest son, which was still in position on Sunday morning when skateborders exploited the challenges of the steps surrounding the statue. (July 2000)

The High Street in Edwardian times, looking south from the junction with Pump Street. The entrance to the market hall was situated under the large clock. The tramlines are now long gone, but even on a Sunday morning this now traffic-free zone is littered with four-wheeled activity: on the right shop-fitting is in busy progress as Worcester's new arcade takes shape, while on the left a lorry, complete with crane, is cleaning the Guildhall's windows. Regrettably, a large tree obscures the view of the rest of the streetscape. (July 2000)

n advertising postcard for Spark & Co., High Street,
ostally used on 30 April 1928. Apparently it was
wice as easy to learn on a Spark piano!' The Worcester
peratic & Dramatic Society, one of the oldest musical
ocieties in Britain, was founded on Spark's premises on
7 February 1892.

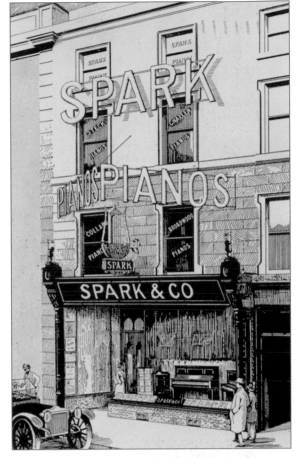

Spark has now given way to a more stark landscape,
and HMV only need (or are allowed) one reference to
their name. At least there is not a tree to hide the
frontage. (July 2000)

The Cross on a postcard published by C.A. Cook – a local stationer – used on 15 April 1914. The Barbourne-bound tram displays an advertisement for the local Spreckley Ales.

The Cross on a postcard published by C.A. Cook, used on 13 May 1910. The tram tracks were laid down in 1904. In the foreground is a horse-drawn omnibus.

A later view of the Cross in the 1920s. The hustle and bustle of this scene was not to last long as the tram tracks were torn up and replaced by buses in 1929.

Master's traditional façade has now been replaced by a nondescript modern version, but superficially at least the streetscape appears relatively unchanged. If you ever have time when next at the Cross look up above the shop windows and compare the incongruous mix of old and new frontages. (July 2000)

Broad Street, near the Cross, on a postcard dating from the Edwardian era. From the right are the shops of George Oliver (boot warehouse), L. Morley (confectioner), Walter J. Beard (grocer), William R. Byron (draper – see next page), and the Metropolitan Bank with its ornate curved windows.

A rather less impressive streetscape now confronts us. The bland Abbey National building stands where the Metropolitan Bank once was, while to its left the HSBC Bank dominates the street scene. (July 2000)

A rare postcard view of William R. Byron's drapery shop at 5 Broad Street, May 1905.

The Benson shoeshop now marks the position of Byron's shop. The frontage has not changed greatly. (July 2000)

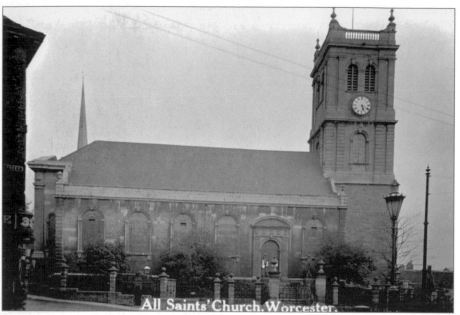

All Saints' church on a postcard published by W.W. Harris, *c.* 1908. The building on the extreme left houses the toy dealership of Miss Mary Ann Partridge, 38 Broad Street.

Today All Saints' stands resplendent, though without the railings that can be seen above. The balustrading on top of the tower has only recently been restored and greatly enhances the appearance of a Georgian church whose interior is well worth seeing. Let us hope that those trees do not grow much larger! (September 2000)

This old engraving shows an attractive black and white building that lay in the shadow of All Saints' church prior to the twentieth century. At one time several other quaint buildings lay in front of the church in a locality known as All Hallows.

In more recent years this has been the site of public lavatories: not an auspicious change of use. (September 2000)

South Quay, *c.* 1902. The tracks of the 'Butt Spur' railway can be seen on the left. The first two buildings on the left are those of Firkins & Co. (hop dealers) and the Severn Iron Warehouse. The boat belongs to George Williams, boat builder, who had premises at 3 South Parade. Beyond the boat are the premises of Courtenay's Worcestershire Sauce Ltd. (part of the site of porcelain manufacture between 1751 and 1840).

Firkins' warehouse has now become residential accommodation, though signs of its past remain: inscribed on the brickwork are the faint painted letters from its time as a hop warehouse. The Severn Iron Warehouse is now the excellent Brown's Restaurant. The name of the Severn Iron Warehouse, however, could be preserved at some future date as it still lurks below the painted lettering of the restaurant.

Reconstruction work on the bridge, South Parade & South Quay, in 1931, pictured by W.W. Dowty. Behind the crane are the premises of Castle Line Steamers whose craft journeyed to Holt Fleet at 2.45 p.m. daily. This bustling scene of activity has been replaced by a much more serene one. Most of the buildings have now been demolished, but at least their replacements are in keeping with the location. (September 2000)

Worcester bridge on a postcard postally used on 25 June 1913, and published by W.W. Harris. The tram on the bridge carries advertisements for the Theatre Royal. The modern view is somehow less interesting and I feel that the old bridge possessed more character. (September 2000)

A 1993 view of Newport Street bus station, which was shortly to be housed within the Crowngate development that was springing up behind it. The scene on a Saturday in July 2000 shows a cluttered mass of cars and wastebins. Considerable imagination will be necessary to improve the environment of this area and others like it. I personally favour the implementation of underground parking, but this is not an option in areas that flood regularly.

The Butts, looking towards the Paul Pry public house, 1993. Little interest has been shown by anyone in preserving the frontages of the buildings in front of the Paul Pry. They are, admittedly, fairly nondescript, but the complete disappearance of buildings such as this from our local townscape seems a pity. Will their replacements blend in well with the public house? Let us hope so, as The Butts is a real mismatch of architectural styles at present. Today's view of this scene shows demolition is not so far away. (June 2000)

A 1993 view of the other side of The Butts, which shows a sorry looking Northwall House standing over an even more forlorn neighbour. The derelict building was duly demolished and replaced by industrial buildings, but fortunately rescue was at hand for Northwall House as our more recent view shows. (June 2000)

The Scala Theatre dominates this view of Worcester's bus centre on a postcard view posted on 19 July 1937. *Shipwreck* was the film showing at that time.

This view shows that the eastern side of Angel Place has not changed much superficially, but the Scala is now a cinematic memory. The buses have been replaced by bustling market stalls that now stand in front of an entrance to part of the modern Crowngate shopping centre – generally considered to be a welcome addition to the city centre townscape. (June 2000)

The Worcestershire Farmers Ltd had a fruit market at the junction with Angel Place and Angel Street, shown here in a photograph by W.W. Dowty. Built in about 1920 it later became the sheep market and more recently held a bustling indoor market, which was moved outdoors to the Corn Market in 1981 (and moved again in recent times to Angel Place, as seen on the previous page). After the removal of the market traders – my own pet food stall included – the building was transformed into the Angel Mall. The location has never proved popular, however, and many businesses failed to make sufficient profits here. Despite overwhelming evidence that shopping was not wanted or viable, council resistance to change of use has been strong. Thankfully, recent plans for a restaurant now look likely to go ahead. (June 2000)

The Theatre Royal, bereft of its magnificent portico, *c*. 1950. The portico unfortunately extended over 5 ft into th
road and had been highly vulnerable to passing lorries. As the car was king, the council ordered its remova
Nowadays they would have pedestrianised the street. Worcester's theatre had been based in Angel Street sin
1781, though the traditional Georgian theatre was largely rebuilt in 1875. Catastrophe occurred on 24 Novemb
1877 when fire completely destroyed the gallery and circle. Rebuilding again took place, but there was to
another fire in 1912 which caused great damage to the stage and auditorium. The theatre was rebuilt yet aga
and managed to survive relatively intact until it was demolished in 1960.

The Theatre Royal, Angel Street *c.* 1912. The iron and glass portico had been added in 1902. Beyond the theatre is the Shakespeare Hotel, Peter's confectionery shop and the woollen warehouse of J.S. Hanson & Son.

Today's Angel Street reveals a tale of lost opportunity. Where there could have been a historic theatre, with its Georgian and Victorian roots, is situated a supermarket building of the most doubtful architectural quality. Fortunately, the Shakespeare Hotel remains, but the building beyond it defies description. (June 2000)

The Foregate pictured on a postcard used on 21 October 1914. This impressive streetscape had not been a feature of Worcester for long; it was only in the 1890s that the eastern side of the Foregate had been demolished in order to widen the road. The entrance to Angel Street is opposite Lennards' shoe shop. Street furniture now breaks up the view; former bus shelters are now in use as a cycle park. The building housing MacDonalds can be seen on the left. The whole view exhibits a pleasant but uneasy mix of old and new; a microcosm of the Worcester that exists in the new century. (2000)

The Berkeley Hospital, situated in the Foregate, on an Edwardian postcard published by W.W. Harris. It was founded by Robert Berkeley of Spetchley who had bequeathed £2,000 in his will for the project. His effigy can be seen above the chapel door. Completed in about 1710, the single-storey almshouses lie either side of the pathway to the chapel.

These almshouses are well preserved and are a real oasis of calm amid a bustling urban environment. The removal of those obscuring trees enables us to appreciate fully the vaguely Flemish feel to this impressive architecture. (July 2000)

The Star Hotel figures prominently on this Kingsway postcard used in 1913. In the far distance the buildings that jut out show how narrow the High Street used to be. Prior to the 1890s the Hopmarket Hotel protruded almost into the middle of the Foregate, resulting in a very narrow thoroughfare.

On a Sunday this scene seems little changed. However, the street line to the left of the road-works was destroyed by the building of Worcester's main post office. Our distant view of the High Street is obscured by trees. (July 2000)

Foregate Street station pictured by J.B. Sherlock, 15 July 1919. Many minor changes have occurred since then, but most noticeable is the removal of the footbridge. Plans are now afoot to change the name of this station in order to enable visitors to establish which of Worcester's stations is centrally situated. Worcester has always had a problem with its railways stations: Foregate Street station is centrally located without parking facilities, while Shrub Hill station is far from the city centre. (July 2000)

The frontage of St Nicholas's church showing the now defunct church steps. St Nicholas's actually dates back to the twelfth century, but was rebuilt in the baroque style during the 1730s. This postcard depicts the proclamation of the death of King Edward VII in 1910.

St Nicholas's has not been used as a church for some years, and it now thrives as a coffee, alcohol and food bar. It is well worth a visit in order to appreciate the size and grandeur of this important local landmark. (June 2000)

Queen Elizabeth's House, The Trinity, *c.* 1910. Its survival as a historic building was secured by great foresight in 1891 when it had to be moved 30 ft on greased railway lines to enable the extension of Trinity Street through to St Nicholas Street. No doubt it would have been knocked down in the 1960s if a similar scheme had been put forward.

Although it is now well preserved, unfortunately, the surrounding buildings tend to dwarf this edifice and reduce its impact. One cannot help but think that it would much rather be sited in Friar Street. (June 2000)

The entrance to The Shambles at its junction with Mealcheapen Street and St Swithins Street, photographed from The Trinity, probably in the 1950s. The black and white building housing J. & F. Hall, ironmongers, was demolished in the early 1960s thanks to the interference of Whitehall, which rejected the local council's plea to retain this building. Foss remained a typical home and garden shop for some years until removing to The Trinity.

J. & F. Hall's replacement was not designed with any thought of fitting in with its illustrious religious neighbour. What a Shambles! (June 2000)

A further view of The Shambles in a postcard view probably published in about 1950. A bustling atmosphere pervades, truly reflecting the scene that many people will remember.

Now The Shambles has a more bland feel to it, pedestrianised and quietened, butchered by progress, but nevertheless a pleasant place to browse and shop. The flower stall helps to add atmosphere to the streetscape, but the young trees look totally inappropriate. (July 2000)

The Shambles on an Edwardian postcard. The Butcher's Arms is aptly named as at least sixteen butchers we then based in this busy thoroughfare: the term 'shambles' indicates their presence, and during the seventeen century there was a butchers' shambles at the southern end of this thoroughfare, a place where country butche could sell their produce. The Butcher's Arms, whose licensee was Henry William Thomas, was situated to the immediate right of the premises of Mrs Jane Winkle, china and earthenware dealer. This old family business is no known as Pratleys. Beyond the Butcher's Arms was the premises of James Shapland, fish and game dealer. The would appear to be another black and white building that would have enhanced the townscape today. On the opposite side of the street are the premises of another butcher, Charles Till junior (extreme right), while two sho beyond, at no. 39, is yet another butcher, Henry Tyler. Sandwiched between these two butchers was a hairdress (note the long barber's pole) and the back entrance to the Old Greyhound public house. This now corresponds The Shambles entrance to the Reindeer Court development.

The Shambles on another Edwardian postcard, seen from further south. The premises of James Shapland jut out into the street in the middle distance. Beyond the Coach and Horses public house (extreme left) is the entrance to the market hall – butter and poultry section. Directly opposite is the entrance to the meat and vegetable section of the market hall.

A much changed scene exists today. Modern stores dominate the High Street side of The Shambles. The rear entrance to the Marks & Spencer store now stands on the site of the Butcher's Arms. The traffic-free environment does not appear to apply on this particular Sunday. (July 2000)

The Corn Market on a postcard that appears to date from the 1920s. As its name indicates, corn was bought and sold here in the nineteenth century and earlier. To the right of Richardson's Stores (formerly the premises of Harry Bromley – see page 117) is the drapery store of Thomas Brown.

The scene today is not all that different. Thankfully all these buildings survive intact even if housing different traders. (June 2000)

The historic King Charles House, situated in the corner of the Corn Market, *c.* 1920. It is a large and complex house with a frontage in New Street as well. This was one of Worcester's major timbered properties. However, I believe that in 1799, or soon after, a fire had ruined much of the building, and a nineteenth-century building was built on the front of it. The old established corn and seed merchants of Holtham & Co. are the neighbours to the right, occupying this newer building. Holtham's later expanded into the part of the building occupied by Charles Collins.

By June 2000 Holtham's had finally given in, victims of the unrelenting competition provided by garden centres and DIY superstores. Beyond Holtham's, in New Street, is the other part of the King Charles House. It has housed a restaurant of the same name for some time now. Interestingly the shop to the left of Holtham's still sells furniture. (June 2000)

The Pheasant Inn, New Street, on an early Edwardian postcard. Henry Griffin was the licensee. The building probably dates back to the late sixteenth century and was not originally a public house. A lady named Eleanor Morris moved to the house in the 1770s, obtained a licence and named the inn the Pheasant. It has also been called the Old Pheasant and, more recently, the Bishop's Rest, but fortunately the original name prevails today. The Pheasant had a bowling green laid down in the late eighteenth century and the now vanished Bowling Green Terrace and Bowling Green Walk were obviously named after this green, which was reserved for the members of the Corporation. Until cockfighting was made illegal in 1800 the Pheasant also held cockfighting events.

The Pheasant thrives today and also looks to be in a fine state of preservation. The building beyond, however, has disappeared. New Street is, together with Friar Street, the best place to make for in order to get an impression of a much older Worcester. (June 2000)

nother fine building in New Street is Nash's House,
ictured here in Edwardian times looking rather
eglected. It dates from the early seventeenth century.
ash's House takes its name from the historically
nportant Nash family who were originally wealthy
othiers. They owned, and lived in, several properties
n New Street. Alderman John Nash's will provided for
charitable hospital, which resulted in the Nash's
lmshouses that can be found in Nash's Passage, just
ff New Street. Both the Pheasant Inn and Nash's
ouse are good examples of close-studded framing and
hallow jetties.

The New Street scene appears more lively and
prosperous today. Numerous restaurants and public
houses enhance the appeal of this street to both local
people and tourists. (June 2000)

The south end of Friar Street, looking towards New Street, *c*. 1908. The small cottages on the left probably date from the early sixteenth century. I had the pleasure of renting one of them in the 1980s, but I am not sure that it was in keeping to make it into a pet shop called Pet Parade. On the right is the historic Greyfriars, perhaps the finest half-timbered edifice in the city. At this time it was in a despoiled state having been converted into shops in about 1870. This now pedestrianised street epitomises the historic heart of Worcester that we should have preserved more completely. The old houses remaining are well preserved, and only beyond Friar Street has a new building intruded (on the corner of New Street with Pump Street). The building that houses Trend of Worcester had a black and white makeover sometime before the 1940s. It is actually unlikely that the old timber-framed buildings of Worcester were originally painted black and white – this was largely a Victorian use of pitch and paint in order to protect old buildings. Greyfriars was thankfully rescued from dereliction and is now owned by the National Trust. (June 2000)

Friar Street, looking southwards, on a postcard used on 21 August 1908. On the right are the uninspiring walls of the Laslett's almshouses, formerly the old city gaol, which was built in the 1820s and contained a treadmill. William Laslett, a successful local solicitor and a Member of Parliament, bought the gaol at auction in 1867 and had the cells adapted to accommodate old married couples.

New almshouses were eventually built in 1912, and they give a much more pleasing aspect to Friar Street. However, the pedestrian zone sign does little to enhance the streetscape. (September 2000)

Tudor House, Friar Street, pictured on a Walter Scott (a national publisher from Bradford, Yorkshire) postcard, *c*. 1936. It probably dates from the second half of the sixteenth century, and was essentially split into three houses. In 1904 the building was in need of repair; its occupants included the Cross Keys public house, a wardrobe dealer and a tinplate worker. Restoration took place in 1909 when many of the original features were found buried under layers of more recent decoration. These features were used by the new occupants, the Tudor Coffee House, to publicise their new concern. However, the local education department had offices here by 1924 so the coffee house had a relatively short period of occupation. This view appears little changed today, but unfortunately the hideous concrete mass of the Lychgate multi-storey car park looms in the background. Tudor House is now a lovely local museum well worthy of a visit. (June 2000)

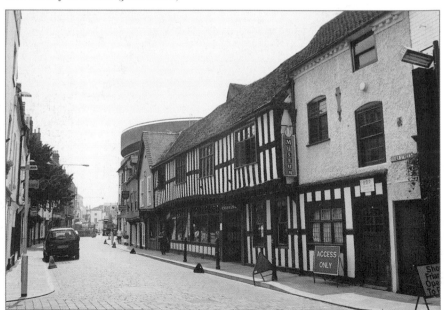

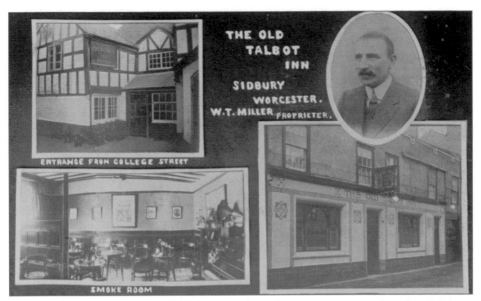

An advertising postcard for The Old Talbot Inn, from the Edwardian period. This is a coaching inn that reputedly dates back to the thirteenth century and is regularly to be found in sixteenth-century records. Until 1835 the Talbot was actually outside the city boundaries in the outlying parish of St Michael's. This made it a convenient place for the county justices to meet. The Old Talbot's address at this time was 51 Sidbury, and it was not on a corner (buildings beyond it were knocked down when Sidbury and College Street were widened). This building, and its name, have been extended and Ye Olde Talbot is now situated on the corner of Friar Street and College Street. The College Street entrance is now obscured by a modern appendage, and the outline of the Lychgate multi-storey car park lurks menacingly in the background. (June 2000)

Ye Olde Talbot appears under siege on 28 June 2000 (above) and 22 September (below) as building work continues apace on the massive new cinema complex on the southern side of Friar Street. However, now the work has been completed this end of Friar Street has been greatly improved. I hope that future plans to refurbish the Lychgate shopping centre will look to further enhance the Friar Street environment.

The antique dealership of W. Underhill was situated at 28 College Street. It would appear that this 1912 photograph, by Percy Parsons, depicts a consignment destined for South Africa. This shop is basically unchanged although now used for a very different purpose. I am afraid I could not find any potential brides to pose outside the shop! (July 2000)

The much-lamented Lich Gate, as viewed from Lich Street, pictured on an Edwardian postcard published by W.W. Harris. Looking through the gate, on the right is the north-east corner of the Cathedral, while on the left is the Punch Bowl Inn. Lich Street at this time was a scene of many historic half-timbered buildings in various states of disrepair. This was an area of the city occupied by labourers, chimney sweeps and glovers. It became ripe for either refurbishment or demolition. Unfortunately the wrong option was chosen and Lich Street and the Lich Gate were lost in the early 1960s as part of the disastrous (historically speaking) Lychgate scheme (why not Lich Gate?). As it is not possible to show the same view now I have taken the photograph below from a location near to the north-east corner of the Cathedral – not, I am afraid, an ideal view to behold from the vicinity of Cathedral. (July 2000)

College Street, on a postcard dated 23 November 1905. The street was not much over 100 years old when this photograph was taken. It was constructed in 1794 in order to cope with the increase in traffic from the south of the city. This had the effect of breaking up the Cathedral precinct. Beyond the Cathedral Wine and Spirit Vaults is the Punch Bowl Inn and St Michael's church. The Lich Gate lay between the church and the Punch Bowl. Beyond the church is the College Café, then run by Mrs M. Parsons, the wife of Percy Parsons (the photographer).

This scene has now changed considerably, replaced by a roundabout and the Lychgate scheme. More greenery, but less character, is the result. (September 2000)

Edgar Tower, Edgar Street, *c.* 1905. Known as St Mary's Gate until the late seventeenth century, it was then named after King Edgar because it was thought that construction took place during his reign in the tenth century. This was the original main gate to the castle and priory. Statuary that had adorned the tower had crumbled away over the course of time, but in 1910 plans were put into effect to replace them.

Edgar Street remains largely intact. However, the recent closure of the King's School tuckshop is revealed by a saleboard on the left. (July 2000)

The bustling thoroughfare of Sidbury pictured on an Edwardian postcard view. This was the widest part of Sidbury just south of the junction with College Street and Friar Street. The two buildings on the extreme right are the Victoria Temperance Hotel and the Angel Commercial Hotel. Most of the buildings on the right were demolished for road widening. Sidbury suffered for many years from traffic congestion and still does. The building that housed the Victoria Temperance Hotel remains intact and is now the Pescatore Restaurant. On the left the City Walls Road has replaced some impressive looking buildings. (September 2000)

The rear of the Commandery when part of the building was used by the well-known local firm of Littlebury's, the printers, *c.* 1908. This view shows the driveway that had been built in 1843 and bisected the Great Hall. Joseph Littlebury, who produced many postcards of the Commandery himself, commented on this as 'vandalism'. The Commandery was founded at the end of the eleventh century as a religious and charitable institution. However, most of the timber-framed buildings would appear to be those that were part of reconstruction work in the late fifteenth century. The Commandery is now the Civil War Centre and a considerable enhancement to Worcester's status as a tourist centre. Fortunately, Littlebury's removed the driveway in 1954 in order to restore the Great Hall to its original state. The large oriel window that helps to light up the Great Hall is no longer obscured by a tree. (July 2000)

St Peter's church was situated at the end of St Peter's Street, which appeared to be endowed with some quaint black and white cottages (demolished in 1950). This postcard, viewed by W.W. Harris, was used in June 1912. St Peter's church had been built in 1836–8 and had replaced a lovely old medieval church. The new church had a much shorter life and, structurally unsound, was demolished in the 1970s.

A completely different scene today, with the motorbikes belonging to the local firm of Skellerns Motorcycles dominating the street. The distant buildings belong to the porcelain works of Royal Worcester. St Peter's Street is yet another example of the failure to protect historic thoroughfares in the postwar period – in this case particularly tragic, in view of the proximity of St Peter's Street to our major tourist attractions. (July 2000)

The rear of the Cathedral Ferry, *c.* 1908. The Water Gate was built in 1378 amid the high stone walls that guarded the city from attack.

A little changed scene today, and although the ferry did not operate for a number of years it has now been resurrected. A board on the right details the operating times. The Water Gate is well worth a visit, as recorded on the sandstone walls are the various heights of Worcester's highest floods. (July 2000)

The Promenade looking northwards towards South Quay and South Parade, *c.* 1936. The absence of riverside trees helps us to appreciate fully the height of the protective walls. The churches of All Saints' and St Andrew's can be seen behind the line of industrial buildings on South Quay. The Promenade has now become Kleve Walk, and luxurious tree growth obscures the Promenade walls and the view beyond. (July 2000)

The view from the Cathedral tower looking northwards along the line of Deansway, *c.* 1935. The derelict area opposite St Andrew's church was the site vacated by the old Worcester firm of Edward Webb and Sons Ltd, horsehair carpet manufacturers, who had removed to Sherriff Street. This was to be the site of the new police station.

The same view today reveals a wealth of changes. The Technical College dwarfs the historic St Alban's church, now used as a day centre, and surrounds the 'Glover's Needle', as St Andrew's spire is often known. On the right of Deansway lies the recently vacated police station. Beyond the police station the Crowngate development dominates the townscape. (September 2000)

The 'Glover's Needle' dominates this view of South Quay and Copenhagen Street. On the corner of Copenhagen Street is St Andrew's Institute, then an important part of the local community. The parish of St Andrew's was densely populated at one time, the maze of streets being permeated by courts of sub-standard housing. South Quay largely consisted of commercial premises.

A much more tranquil scene now prevails. Few people now live in this area of Worcester, which is dominated by gardens, a car park, and a complex road system that defies all logic. Controversy has raged recently over the ill-fated 'Millennium Quayhead' scheme; regardless of the rights or wrongs of the situation I find it rather galling that no one thought to plan something that would have celebrated the industrial and commercial links with the past that exist here. (September 2000).

The view of the city centre from the Cathedral. Thankfully the modern skyline in this view is still dominated
the historic churches and older brick buildings. Of the churches in view, however, only Sansome Street Bap
church is now in regular religious use. A visit to the top of the Cathedral tower is an extremely worthwi
experience; make it a resolution to climb to the top as soon as possible. The physical exercise alone is exhilarati
(September 2000)

2

The Suburbs East of the Severn

Suburban growth in Worcester has accelerated considerably over recent years. To the north of the city centre earlier expansion into the parishes of Barbourne, St Stephen's and Claines has been somewhat piecemeal with no large areas of estate housing, the Blanquettes development excepted. The area directly to the east of the city centre has been developed haphazardly with large swathes of the older Worcester being swept away, and even now traditional buildings, such as the Beehive public house, face an uncertain future. Further to the east vast housing estates have been built with little regard to major road access to the city centre, while the southern area of the city has been transformed by the large St Peter's housing development.

Elephants never forget their kerb drill apparently. This procession, with Shrub Hill station in the background, probably dates back to the 1950s.

This is now a very busy road junction where your kerb drill is governed by traffic lights. Elgar House, one of Worcester's ugliest office buildings, conceals the façade of Shrub Hill station. (July 2000)

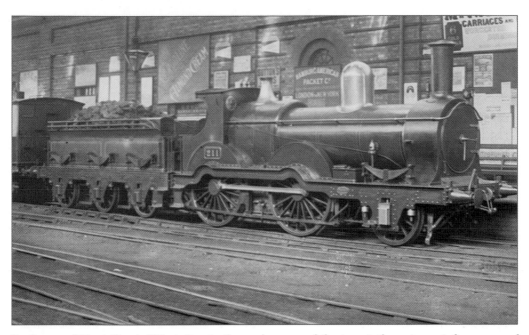

Engine no. 211 at Shrub Hill station in the early years of the twentieth century. A fine array of posters can be seen on the platform walls.

Stations seemed to be much more atmospheric and busy places in bygone years; this photograph conveys the blandness of the current Shrub Hill scene. (July 2000)

The 'Vinegar Line' crossing and signals in Shrub Hill Road. The large corrugated building was owned by the engineering firm of Heenan & Froude. In the distance is the since demolished Prince of Wales public house. (June 1956)

The 'Vinegar Line' disappeared in the 1960s as our 'Wimbledon Fortnight' photograph shows. This is now a scene of billiard balls – the American pool bar Suzy – and a tennis ball – the bill poster, top right, features Anna Kournikova's endorsement of a shock absorber bra with the slogan 'Only the ball should bounce'. (June 2000)

Mona Villa, 21 Albany Road, is a typical Victorian property in suburban Worcester. This early twentieth-century postcard, taken by A. & G. Colwell, reveals the ornate railings typical of the period. At this time Albany Road was home to numerous railway workers, Shrub Hill station and the extensive railway yards being only a short stroll away.

Our recent photograph reveals a change typical of our times: the removal of the front garden and wall to make way for our treasured motor car. In this case there was even room for a garage. Necessary, I know, but perhaps not so aesthetically appealing. (July 2000)

The corner of Till Street and Lansdowne Road in Edwardian times. This was then the limit of suburban growth, no notable housing occurring until after the junction of Lansdowne Road with Laslett Street. Merriman's Hill was an area of pasture and orchards.

Now the railings and wall have been replaced, and a young skateboarder has appeared on the scene. Till Street is no longer on the edge of the city, but areas of greenery may still be found close by. (July 2000)

Droitwich Road pictured on a postcard dated 21 October 1910. The outlook was a pleasant one, as on the opposite side of the road were the nurseries of W.B. Rowe & Son. This view was taken from the junction with Bilford Lane (now Bilford Road), which was not yet a crossroads as Coombs Road was yet to be built.

A little-changed scene awaiting the grandiose park and ride scheme. Will they yet find room for a bus-only lane? Don't hold your breath. (June 2000)

Claines Fruit & Vegetable Gardens operated from this house on the Ombersley Road, *c.* 1908; the postcard was produced by Pitt & Son, Park Avenue. At this time housing beyond the junction with Checketts Lane was concentrated almost exclusively on the eastern side of the road. For many years this has been the location of a grocer's and petrol station (George R. Smalley in 1953, and Grantham's more recently).

Alas, the old-fashioned pumps have now gone and a modern sales and service station is now operated by Mark Grantham. (June 2000)

Northwick Road also saw suburban growth in Victorian times. Housing extended in a linear pattern on the eastern side of the road as far as the junction with Saunders Street. Little housing could be found on the western side, though some is featured here (looking northwards), close to the junction with Union Place in about 1908. The old hamlet of Northwick was centred on the small triangular green which still exists at the junction with Old Northwick Lane. Now only the Northwick Arms and the distant house remain. The entrance to Faithful Overalls is on the left, opposite the junction with Vine Street. Beyond Faithful Overalls the minor side road of Neweys Hill now leads to a small housing development. (June 2000)

Park Avenue pictured in the Edwardian period by Mrs J. Pitt & Son, who operated from 2 Park Avenue (Milford Villas), situated at the junction with Ombersley Road. This view looks eastwards from a point near the Redcliffe Street junction. Park Avenue was presumably named after Barbourne Park, a large area of parkland stretching from Barbourne Brook to the Kepax Ferry, and from the main road to the river. Gheluvelt Park is the remaining part of the old pleasure grounds. A new housing development has now appeared on the land formerly owned by Severn Trent. (June 2000)

The old water tower at the end of Tower Road, *c.* 1908, when occupied by Mr Henry Jarman, an artist. This was Worcester's waterworks from around 1770 until it was replaced in 1858. Unfortunately it was demolished in the 1960s.

Now, as we look from the old waterworks buildings towards Tower Road, the new and aptly named Riverside housing development is rapidly appearing. The site of the water tower is now preserved for posterity, although flooded when this photograph was taken. (November 2000)

Gheluvelt Park featured on a postcard used on 11 July 1931. The park was opened in the 1920s and was named after the Battle of Gheluvelt, Belgium, fought on 31 October 1914, where the Worcestershire Regiment displayed great heroism. The trees have now matured, giving a more enclosed feel to the park in high summer. (June 2000)

St George's Square, *c.* 1908, is a superb setting for a church which has changed relatively little since being built in the 1890s. It replaced a far simpler church that had been built in 1829. The new building was designed by Sir Aston Webb, a distinguished London-born architect, who married Maria, daughter of Dr Everett of Foregate Street, in 1876. St George's School was initially based in the square during Victorian times but soon moved to new buildings in St George's Lane North. St George's Laundry, the well-known old Worcester firm, was situated just to the left of the church. On the modern view the street furniture is different and cars have inevitably become part of the view. (July 2000)

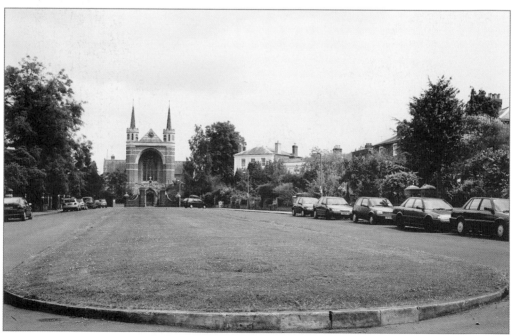

Barbourne Road looking northwards, *c.* 1908. On the right is a fine example of an early eighteenth-century terrace, known as Paradise Row, which incorporates the Talbot Hotel. The scene is dominated by the tall Spreckley Brewery building.

Numerous changes are now detectable. On the extreme left the building occupied by Richardson's Stores Ltd (grocers) in 1908 has made way for the widening of Hebb Street. The majestic and forbidding brewery building has long since gone. Fortunately, we cannot see its replacement in this view. The terrace on the right now seems shorter as a result of the Talbot Hotel being given a black and white facelift. The inevitable bus lane has appeared in order to confuse people who dare to drive their cars into the city. (July 2000)

Worcester Royal Grammar School, The Tything, *c*. 1924, photographed by Percy Parsons. This is one of the oldest schools in the country, although we do not know when it was originally founded; it was certainly in operation by the thirteenth century, but may be even older. The school moved to the Upper Tything site in about 1868 and has expanded greatly since then. Apart from the railings this is an essentially unchanged view, although the Eld Hall was heavily clad in scaffolding. (July 2000)

t Mary Magdalene's church as viewed from St Mary's
treet on a postcard, published by W.W. Harris, dated
5 September 1911. Behind the church, in Northfield
treet, was St Mary's Infants' Day School and Sunday
chool. Northfield Street seems much wider than it
eally is.

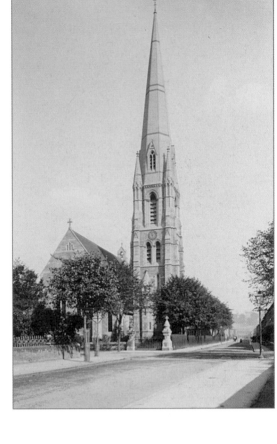

St Mary's is no longer in use as a church but is well
preserved in the form of luxury flats. The trees in
1911 seemed to blend into the scene better than
they do now. (June 2000)

Austin House, Castle Street, *c.* 1950. Built by J. Soutar in 1939 on the site of the old prison, this was, perhaps, the major garage and showroom in Worcester for many years. The church in the distance is the long since demolished Presbyterian Christchurch.

Fortunately, Austin House has been recognised as an architecturally interesting building, and is now used as a carpet and furniture warehouse. The building beyond is to be a new police station and magistrates' court – a modern design of considerable architectural merit that blends in well with its surviving Georgian neighbours. (July 2000)

The Infirmary on a postcard posted on 11 November 1904, and published by Burrow's of Cheltenham. The view is dominated by the then new ornate entrance gates and railings, donated by Lord Beauchamp, serving as the entrance to Pitchcroft.

The fine Georgian architecture of the original Infirmary, designed by Anthony Keck, is now obscured by the modern extensions. However, the Infirmary is now due for closure, and ambitious new schemes are looming for this site. Let us hope that Keck's building will be treated more sympathetically with regards to its surroundings when plans come to fruition. (July 2000)

Worcester has a fine tradition of fêtes and carnivals. This is the Railway Mission Cart, photographed by Pe
Parsons, at the Band of Hope Union Fête and Gala, 4 August 1908. It was decorated in red, white and blue, a
not surprisingly, it won first prize for display in the parade.

A decorated float prepares to leave Pitchcroft at the Worcester Carnival procession, 15 July 2000. No prizes for spotting the spelling mistake! There was no carnival procession in 2001 because of a lack of entrants. This was partly owing to, I am afraid to say, the treatment the float participants received in reward for their efforts in 2000, when their movements were restricted unnecessarily by security staff, preventing them from access to their own seats. 'Never again' was the oft-repeated phrase. I actually fared better than the people who should have been allowed through to the start of the carnival procession by posing as an official photographer.

Glove manufacturing was on of the main local industries many years (the Glovers' Company was incorporated early as 1497). Most famous of these were Dent, Allcroft & Co. Firkins & Co. and Fowne Bros & Co. The company of I. & R. Morley were situated the top of Sunnyside Road from around 1920 onwards. This entry for a carnival procession is undated.

The rural crisis is highlighted on this carnival float seen at Pitchcroft on 15 July 2000. Political correctne prevents me from controversial comment, other than to say that things are not getting better, and that, as general rule, the town seems to be replacing the countryside. Since last year's parade farming and rural business have been devastated by the foot and mouth epidemic.

Barry Street, situated in the Arboretum, pictured on a postcard dated 23 March 1909. It was photographed by Max Fischer, who had premises at 33 Lowesmoor. The fields beyond were to become allotments. The shop on the corner of Lowell Street was a small grocer's operated by H.W. Tyler.

The Arboretum thrives today as a close-knit community. Unfortunately, the shop (in the 1970s known as the Dog Shop, that offering a dog-clipping service) has now been converted into a house. (July 2000)

A funeral party at Astwood Cemetery, photographed by A. & G. Colwell, in the spring of 1910.

The arched entrance and ornate railings were removed many years ago, and there is now a less austere feel to the surroundings. A one-way system now operates within the cemetery; this is an exit only. (July 2000)

The remains of Lyppard Grange in 1992. This was a lovely local house that suffered dreadful neglect for many years, despite local pleas for its restoration. By 1992 it would appear the situation was too far gone, but like a phoenix from the ashes a new public house has arisen, named after its predecessor. Part of the grounds, including a small lake, remain, and the local community centre and a large supermarket are close by. (June 2000)

St Catherine's Hill, London Road, on a pre-First World War postcard taken by A. & G. Colwell. The Revd Edward Gilliat was the house's owner. At one time many large houses such as this, together with their spacious grounds, surrounded the centre of the city. They often became the victims of suburban growth. In this case the house was demolished to make way for the cul-de-sac aptly named St Catherine's Hill built in the 1920s and 1930s. However, the original entrance survives despite the attentions of graffiti louts. (July 2000)

The spacious grounds of St Catherine's Hill contained a grass tennis court. The terraced housing of Victoria Avenue can be seen beyond the tennis court, while Perry Wood can be seen in the far distance.

A portion of the grounds were sold off at the beginning of the twentieth century in order to build a church for the local community. St Martin's church was dedicated in June 1911. (July 2000)

A general view of Battenhall, showing Battenhall Mount and its lodge, *c.* 1908. Battenhall has always been a highly desirable area of Worcester in which to live. At this time many of the local entrepreneurs had their homes here, including G.A. Theodore Littlebury (Littlebury & Co.) and Percy Townshend (T.S. Townshend & Sons – the well-known millers).

It is now impossible to recreate the picture above because of the trees obscuring the view. The lodge, however, can be shown in fine fettle. The banner is advertising St Mary's Convent School's annual fête. (July 2000)

St Mark's church, Orchard Street, Cherry Orchard, *c.* 1925. The church was built in 1903 at a cost of £2,000. Miss Jane Darke gave £1,000 for improvements to the building and to establish a small endowment. This is a view that has not changed greatly. The Cherry Orchard development was the first major suburban incursion into this area of Worcester that had, in Victorian times, been a rural idyll. (July 2000)

The Ketch Inn, Bath Road, pictured on a postcard dated 5 July 1909. F. Partridge was the licensee, and possessed pleasure gardens that extended down to the Severn. The writer of the postcard complains: 'We have caught no fish today, but I am in good spirits.' I am not too certain what spirits he means! The Ketch dates back many centuries, and, reputedly, Cromwell's army supped their ale here. The name comes from a typical Severn sailing vessel. The Ketch is now a very different pub, but at least, thankfully, the name has been retained. With the considerable expansion of the St Peter's estate a flourishing future seems assured for this old pub. (June 2000)

3

The Suburbs West of the Severn

This area of Worcester is traditionally known as St John's, but it also encompasses Lower Wick, Dines Green and Henwick. The central part of St John's possesses a real sense of community and is now familiarly known as 'the village within the city'. Not too many historic buildings have been lost here, while sub-standard housing in the area of Tybridge Street was swept away in the 1960s. Multi-storey flats, erected on part of the cleared site, tower uncomfortably above their smaller neighbours. The expanding population and increased traffic within St John's is now creating local discord as pressure for improved supermarket facilities grows. Those wishing to retain the viability of the 'village within the city' will, in my view, need to accept that new shopping facilities need to be placed close to the heart of St John's; provision of these elsewhere will kill off the historic shopping centre as people are diverted from old habits.

Cripplegate Park was opened in 1922 according to the plaque on the fountain. Samuel Southall performed the opening ceremony, but he was to be upstaged somewhat in 1932 by the Prince of Wales, later King Edward VIII. The building to the right of the fountain in the middle distance is that of the long-since demolished Bridge Mills, where sawing, planing and moulding took place. The park has now matured and tennis courts lie beyond the fountain. (June 2000)

The entrance to Cripplegate Park pictured on a postcard dated 6 July 1936. Cripplegate Park was extended in the early 1930s, which explains why it was apparently opened in both 1922 and 1932 (the 1932 plaque refers to the extension, which was opened by the Prince of Wales). In the middle distance is the long-gone Hounds Lane School.

To replicate the view accurately now is not possible because of tree growth, but a nearby view seems to consist of a mixture of churches and street furniture. (September 2000)

The entrance to Worcester tramway depot, possibly about 1910. A horse-drawn tramway service had started in Worcester in 1881, but this depot was converted to accommodate electric cars in about 1903. Electric cars commenced operation on 6 February 1904. Trams ceased operating in Worcester in 1928, but the depot was used for industrial purposes (notably Windshields of Worcester) until the 1970s. The depot was demolished in 1978 and now the site is home to the Co-op supermarket. Schemes for a more grandiose supermarket within St John's now cast doubts over its future, although recent refurbishment would indicate a long-term commitment. (September 2000)

A rare view of St John's, *c.* 1940. Postcards of this period are unusual because of the economies made necessary by the outbreak of the Second World War. The shops from the left are those of Newman's (fruiterer), Fudger (a butcher's – now Narraway's), and J.H. Tyler (wireless engineer).

The streetline appears well preserved sixty years later, and The Bell public house has not been renamed. (July 2000)

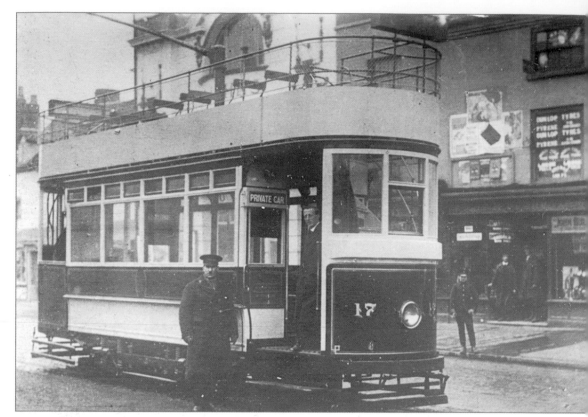

Tram car no. 17 pictured in front of St John's Cinema, *c.* 1922. This was the route between the Cross and Malvern Road (terminating at the Brunswick Arms). Trams ran at ten-minute intervals throughout most of the day on this particular route. Tram car nos 16 and 17 were the last to be provided for the Worcester Electric Traction Co. They arrived in 1922 and were slightly larger than the rest of the fleet. When the Worcester tramway system closed in 1928 they were sold to the Cheltenham and District Light Railway. The cinema was run by the Godsell brothers at this time.

he cinema has not shown films since about 1959 and was derelict for a long period. It has, at times, been a ibrant nightclub, or so I'm told. These properties now face an uncertain future as argument rages over planned upermarket developments. (June 2000)

St John's Green, Bransford Road, *c.* 1908. This was the site of a fair, usually called St John's Hiring Fair or Mop, until the 1870s. A toll house once stood on the corner of Bransford Road and Malvern Road and this helped to enclose the green. Although Bransford Road was the original horse tram route the electrified trams used the Malvern Road instead. The 'green' area now provides parking for shoppers while the building to the far left on our older view has disappeared. (June 2000)

Happy Land North pictured on a postcard dated 6 November 1913. The quaint and unusual name is said to derive from the success of a sand and gravel pit that previously stood there; it certainly proved very profitable for its owners as they were then able to build the small Happy Land housing development. The public house on the corner of Happy Land West and Bromyard Road was aptly named the Sandpits Inn (now the Bedwardine).

The traditional wall and railings have gone and, apart from a local shortage of car parking space, this still seems a tranquil spot. (September 2000)

The Dog and Duck Ferry in flood as viewed from Ferry Bank, St John's. This was probably a summer flood in the earlier years of the twentieth century, possibly that of June 1924. The ferry takes its name from the Dog and Duck Inn which must have been situated on the St John's side of the ferry.

The ferry in flood again: the height of the flood seems similar. The inevitable street furniture intrudes at this quiet and tranquil spot just yards from the busy Henwick Road. (November 2000)

Hylton Road in flood during December 1910, photographed by W.T. Clutterbuck. The view is probably looking away from the railway arches northwards. This part of Hylton Road has now disappeared completely.

Hylton Road in flood, looking towards the railway arches. Amphibious cars are for sale at the Monarch Used Car Centre. The houses on the left date from the early 1890s onwards. (November 2000)

Henwick station, as photographed by J.B. Sherlock, on 15 July 1919. This was a fully-staffed station with its own booking office, waiting room, stationmaster's office and porter service. The station was demolished in the late 1960s although the signal box remains.

This site is now over-ripe for development, but plans for a nursing home now seem likely to go ahead. Whatever does happen I'm sure that in years to come everyone will be wondering why it was not reopened as a railway station/park and ride scheme. (June 2000)

St Clement's church, as viewed from the Henwick level crossing, on a postcard dated 19 April 1911. St Clement's church was built in 1823 in the unusual Neo-Norman style, making it quite different in appearance to any other local church.

Our view of this church has now been affected by a somewhat inappropriate housing development. The Norman feel of this church has been considerably reduced by the absence of the rather striking pinnacles. I wonder where they have gone. A continental-style barrier has now replaced the more traditional crossing gates. (June 2000)

4

Rural Surroundings

The distinction between town and country continues to blur. Hamlets and villages close to the city find themselves enveloped by spreading urban tentacles. Even where green fields intervene between city and village, the lack of real separation produces an impression of village suburban life. Fortunately, villagers rebel against the insidious growth of urbanism by maintaining the principles of village life through local churches, clubs and voluntary organisations. Keeping the local public house, post office and shop is a vital prerequisite in maintaining local identity. The above postcard, in the early twentieth century featuring a rifle club at their licensed meeting place (can you guess where?), illustrates a bygone rural comradeship.

The Fox Inn, Bransford, *c.* 1908, on a postcard published by W.W. Harris. Situated on the main Worcester–Hereford road, there was no regular bus service at this time, but carriers served Bransford on Wednesdays and Saturdays. This is where the Fox rifle club photograph was taken: three members of the Portman family are featured. Bransford was rather a split parish in Edwardian times, with the Fox and the post office being situated at Bransford Bridge while the chapel and the railway station were over a mile away.

The Fox is now a much larger establishment with extensive children's facilities. Unfortunately, it is prone to flooding and suffered greatly during the floods of 2000. This view also shows a new dwelling named the Old Bridge Cottage. (June 2000)

Powick, *c.* 1904. On the left is the local butcher's, while the horse and cart are outside the premises of Walter S. Knott, shopkeeper and postmaster.

Powick suffers as a community as it is split by the busy Worcester–Malvern road. Nevertheless, it still has a thriving butcher's shop (C.J. Partridge), while beyond the van is the local post office stores and off licence. (June 2000)

The Lodge, Powick Asylum, *c.* 1908. In the *Littlebury's Directory* for that year it was described as the 'Worcester County and City Lunatic Asylum', and was situated in Asylum Lane. Such terminology would not be acceptable these days.

The site of the hospital is now a large housing development, but fortunately the historic lodge building is well preserved. Powick now has fairly large housing areas within its bounds and is very much a typical dormitory village. (June 2000)

Callow End's post office in Edwardian times was a rather humble affair. Its superior thatched neighbour survives, as do both the house beyond and the Old Bush public house. The post office has since moved location, but it at least remains in operation. Many other villages have lost one of their vital lifelines with the closure of rural post offices. Unlike Powick, Callow End manages to achieve isolation from the hustle and bustle of the nearby city. (June 2000)

The main road through Kempsey, *c.* 1909. In the distance is a horse-drawn bus bound for Worcester. The shop on the right is that of Edwin Douglas, pastry cook.

Some thirty or so years later the same bus service was run by Midland Red. The shop that lay between The Talbot public house and the house on the corner has disappeared.

The vacant lot was eventually bought to provide an extension to the Talbot, as can be seen in this view. The corner house is still intact but in urgent need of renovation and redecoration. The cottage on the left is one of the few remaining thatched cottages left in Kempsey. (June 2000)

A slightly different view on the same day. The public house virtually opposite the Talbot is now named the Walter de Cantelupe Inn (formerly the Queen's Head). Kempsey is a large village that has successfully maintained its own identity. Despite its proximity to the city it retains a variety of shops and public houses.

Another main road public house in Kempsey is the Crown, pictured here by Percy Parsons, *c.* 1910.

The same view today reveals a similar scene. Both the pub and the shop (The Original Stores) survive. The Crown has undergone considerable change, however. The recent reduction of the speed limit through the village has helped to improve the environment. (June 2000)

Norton Barracks, pictured by W.W. Harris in the Edwardian era. This was the home of the Worcestershire Regiment from 1881 to 1962; about 200 men were on site at this time.

The barracks has now been transformed into a modern housing estate, but fortunately the historic gatehouse has been preserved to serve as a reminder of the illustrious past of the Worcestershire Regiment, as do the roads of the estate, which are aptly named after famous battles the regiment was involved in. The village of Norton is still somewhat isolated from the barracks development, which is yet another example of Worcester's unabating urban growth. (June 2000)

The village of Stoulton on a postcard used in 1906. The tower of St Edmund's church can be seen in the background. Edwardian Stoulton was a relatively small village, having a population of around 320 (including the hamlets of Hawbridge, Windmill Hill and Wolverton).

All of the houses still exist today, but, alas, the busy A44 road intrudes on the tranquillity of this spot. (June 2000)

The schoolchildren of Stoulton proudly pose for the camera just prior to the outbreak of the First World War. This postcard was used on 24 July 1914, just twenty-six days after the assassination of Archduke Ferdinand at Sarajevo, and a few days before the British entered the fray. In the background is the horse and cart belonging to Harry Bromley, an oil and lamp dealer, based originally at 7 Silver Street, Worcester, and subsequently at 1 Corn Market.

To recreate the group photograph these days would be nigh impossible as traffic hurtles through Stoulton. The rural idyll has now been replaced by a garage. (June 2000)

The Croome Hunt meet at Upton Snodsbury, photographed by W.T. Clutterbuck in April 1909. The Coventry Arms, whose licensee was John Warner, can be seen in the background. The population of Upton Snodsbury, together with Cowsden, was around 300 at this time.

The busy A422 lies in front of the Coventry Arms, which like so many country pubs relies on serving food in order to prosper. The haystack has been replaced by a conservatory. (June 2000)

A traditional thatched cottage in Crowle, photographed by W.W. Harris during the early 1900s. Although this looked an idyllic place in which to live, the reality was probably somewhat different. The population of Crowle, together with Sale Green, was around 550 at this time.

These cottages are now well preserved within a slightly larger village, which remains aloof from Worcester because of its location on a minor road. (June 2000)

Tibberton canal as seen from the bridge, looking northwards, in the 1950s. The scene is populated by people and cars, but no barges are in view. The village of Tibberton is largely situated south of the canal and is basically of a linear pattern. Like Crowle, Tibberton is situated on a minor road and seems remote from Worcester. It also possesses those vital attributes of a school, post office and public houses.

By contrast, brightly painted barges dominate the same spot in this more recent photograph. The increased popularity of canal holidays provides the village with extra revenue. (June 2000)

The Tibberton canal bridge, as seen from the north, on a postcard dated 28 August 1936.

This is a little-changed scene apart from the proliferation of undergrowth. (29 June 2000)

A superb study of the main village street through Ombersley, *c*. 1906, photographed by the skilled J. White of Kidderminster. The premises of W.H. King, plumber, glazier and painter, are prominent. This was the original Charity School House founded in 1729. Edwardian Ombersley was an important village and the large parish (including the hamlets of Dunhampton, Sytchampton, Hawford, Hadley, Chatley, Uphampton, Comhampton, Acton, Lineholt, Boreley, and Oldfield) had a population of over 2,000. Black and white tranquillity still prevails, as fortunately the busy A449 road bypasses the village. Ombersley possesses great vitality, with high-quality shops, public houses and restaurants to accompany the basics of traditional village life. (June 2000)

The Holt Fleet Hotel, late 1930s. Holt Fleet has been a popular weekend haunt for holidaymakers from the industrial areas of the West Midlands for many years. Not too far from their homes, but a million miles away in terms of environment, offering the rural dream combined with good fishing and boating. Hop-pickers were also drawn here in large numbers. Steamer trips were a major attraction here and brought many daytrippers to the hotel. The hotel was replaced and enlarged after the Second World War, with a less interesting building, I am sure you will agree. (June 2000)

The Red Lion, Holt Heath, *c.* 1910. Thomas Pitt was the licensee at this time; he catered for picnic parties and cyclists (boasting a lock-up cycle shop), and also offered good stabling. The population of Holt was around 300 at this time. Holt's post office and school were based in Holt Heath, but Holt church is some distance away, perched high above the Severn, close to Holt Castle.

The Red Lion's unusual frontage is now more prominent, as are the road junction and signposts. Holt Heath still has a post office, but the school has disappeared (children now travel to Grimley). Modern housing now dominates the village that has been developed rather haphazardly. (June 2000)

The green at Hallow, looking towards Church Lane, *c.* 1920, in a photograph by Percy Parsons. The house on the left (Sigston) was subsequently extended and then was split into two properties. Recently, however, it has been refurbished and returned to its original state. The tree that now obscures Sigston was planted in June 1953 to commemorate the coronation of Queen Elizabeth II. While some of the cottages in the lane remain others have gone. The see-saw is still a feature of the village green. Hallow has close connections with Worcester, but possesses a strong community spirit as well as thriving local facilities. (June 2000)

The green, looking northwards, *c.* 1910, photographed by Percy Parsons. Bright white fencing surrounds the recently erected black and white cottages which were built through the benevolence of Mrs C. Wheeley Lea. To the right is the home of John Clay, plumber, glazier and paperhanger, while the building to the far right was, at about this time, the village post office. The cottage behind the tree set in railings has since been demolished.

Trees now dominate the green in summer, obscuring the Lea cottages that now lack attractive fencing. (June 2000)

Broadheath bakery and the Bell Inn photographed by Percy Parsons, *c.* 1925. The local brewery of Spreckley's provided the ales for F. Hayward to sell. Broadheath only became a separate ecclesiastical parish in 1910 (formed from parts of Hallow, Wichenford, and St John Bedwardine). The church was erected in 1904 by public subscription.

All the buildings still survive and are now painted white. The shop on the left is the local post office and village store. The Bell Inn serves Banks's Ales. Lower Broadheath has become a dormitory village and thrives accordingly. (June 2000)

Finally, I feel I should atone for my earlier irreverence to Sir Edward Elgar. Above is an Edwardian postcard (published by W.W. Harris) of Elgar's birthplace at Upper Broadheath, while below is its new neighbour, the Elgar centre. I can thoroughly recommend a visit to this superb museum. (June 2000)